Cold Night Lullaby

Colin Mackay

For the Aid Workers of the World

Cold Night Lullaby

Colin Mackay

Chapman Publishing

1998

Chapman Publishing
4 Broughton Place
Edinburgh EH1 3RX
Scotland

The publisher acknowledges an award from
the Deric Bolton Trust towards the publication
of this volume.
The publisher acknowledges the financial assistance
of the Scottish Arts Council.

A catalogue record for this volume is
available from the British Library.
ISBN 0-906772-86-9

Chapman New Writing Series
Editor Joy Hendry
ISSN 0953-5306

Some of these poems have appeared in the following magazines:
*Anarchist Angel, Bardonni/Stopgap, Candelabrum,
Cencrastus, Chapman, Christian Poetry Review, Envoi, First Time,
Other Poetry, Poet's Voice, Red Herring, Understanding, Vigil.*
'Bosnian Elegy' appeared in the Mekler & Deahl
1997 anthology *Doors of the Morning.*

Cover design: Deborah Cumming
Author photograph: John Doyle

Printed by
Inglis Allen
Middlefield Road
Falkirk FK2 9AG

Contents

Introduction

Earlier this year I listened to an impassioned philosopher quoting a survivor of the Auschwitz death camps: "From now on theology can only be taken seriously if it is done in the presence of burning children."

I didn't know then that six weeks later I would find myself in Auschwitz standing by the ovens where children had burned. The survivor's words came back to me as they did again so forcefully when I read this vital collection of poems. In truth, Mackay's bitter address to God in the poem 'You Mock Us' goes to the heart of the proposition – and to the heart of darkness.

Mackay's journeys are journeys into hell, into the hell of what was done to Bosnia and of what Bosnia did to itself as the world looked on; into the hell of what happened to those the poet met and those he did not meet; into the hell of those he travelled with, those he cared for and those he loved. It is also about what Bosnia did to him.

But this book also raises the further thought that poetry itself can only be taken seriously if it too is done in the presence of burning children. And if there are any readers who still suffer from the notions of there being material unsuited to poetry, then this is not the book for them – though perhaps it should be.

On a first reading you might be tempted to argue that there are a few poems which could have been excised by a more rigorous editing because they seem to repeat fire or are hitting the same target from different angles. But that is to miss the point. This book has to be read as a complete, human document and it has to be read in its entirety, preferably at one sitting.

It is a personal odyssey of pain and suffering, of faith and doubt, of anger, hate, love and confusion. It is also a book which will affect you deeply; at least make you stop and think – and, perhaps more importantly, stop to feel.

It may well be that, as Auden said, poetry changes nothing. But the impetus of Mackay's writing would seem to want to give the lie to that assertion. In that lives its hope.

If, on the other hand, we say with Orwell that all art is propaganda in any case, then Mackay's poetry is 'propaganda' for the pitiful and tragic truth of the human condition as well as being by its very nature a plea for dignity and understanding, for cultural and racial tolerance and for the humanising of all politics.

Mackay was a poet, and a fine poet, before he ever set foot on Bosnian soil. And this is why perhaps he can distil for us so lucidly the spirit of his experiences there. His poetry is reinforced, and transformed, by his subsequent experience.

But this is not a book of 'war poetry' as it is normally understood. Mackay was not a combatant in a 'regular' war. He was a volunteer, humanitarian aid worker faced with that most awful of wars – civil war – where neighbour turns on neighbour and lifelong friends and colleagues turn to rapine, to torture and even to mass slaughter.

This is a testament that should be read by everyone from students of theology and philosophy to ideologues and politicians of all orders. It is a document for holocaust studies and a plea to all on this small planet to look, listen and learn.

It has poems of rare beauty, oases of light and hope on the darkening plain.

It is a painful book. It is a healing book. Above all, it is a book that had to be written and one that has to be read.

Raymond Ross

Foreword

The war in Bosnia had been raging for weeks and months when we got there. It had been kindling for years and decades before that, but I am neither journalist nor historian, and this is not the place to talk of the causes of things. These poems are about effects: the effect of a bullet on the body, the effect of fear and hope upon the human heart.

People came to Bosnia from many places, and doubtless for many reasons, but pity was the great determiner. They were a Foreign Legion without guns, an International Brigade without self-righteousness. Call them the footsoldiers of reconciliation and you would not be far wrong. Some of them died there, including one I knew. I have called him 'Johnny'. It was not the name he had on the voters' role but that is of no consequence. His real name was Everyman.

And Bosnia's real name? She was a beautiful mountain country, she had green hills and meadows, woods and tumbling rivers. She was very like Scotland. Village after village of whitewashed walls and red-tiled roofs waxed in beauty with the summer sun. Her people watched satellite television and drove Fiats and Renaults. It was all so peaceful, so civilised, and only three days drive from London, yet the things that happened there were medieval in their brutality.

Bosnia was like Naphtali in the Bible, she was both lovely and a land lost in darkness. She was the Pool of Siloam and the Valley of the Shadow of Death. Call her Everywhere.

On our journey through that land we experienced many

things, both good and bad, fine and ugly, and some that were all of these. Eventually we came to a village. There was a woman there, her name was Svetlana. She was a widow with two young children called Ahmad and Ludmilla, and she was a Serb, a Christian of the Orthodox faith. The village was Muslim. It had driven its Serbs out over the Drina river, though Muslim and Serb had lived there together since before its oldest inhabitants were born. They let Svetlana stay out of respect, because her husband had been a Muslim who had been killed fighting for Bosnian independence.

I thought that showed a chink of light in the darkness of their hate, and that where there was light there was hope and life. But then I still did not know what hate could do. On the other side of the river were Serbian fighters breathing vengeance. The morning came when we drove to Sarajevo to arrange passage for Svetlana and her children on an outgoing flight. When we returned that afternoon, it was a place of corpses.

The Serbs, who had killed everyone, including babies, had reserved their greatest hatred for the Serbian woman they doubtless regarded as a traitor and a whore. Svetlana had been butchered. Ludmilla, six years old, was dead beside her with her brains blown out. Ahmad had disappeared.

Years later, I still cannot describe it.

Eventually we returned.

It is difficult to find anything new to say about the horrors of war that has not been said since the greatest disillusioning of 1914. Perhaps it just needs to be said again and again. I have tried to say a little of it here, however inadequately.

There are those who cannot believe in a loving God because of the cruelties that happen in the world, and there are those who can only endure these cruelties because they believe in a loving God. I will not judge. I only know that part of us all died there in Bosnia, and we suffered grief that we had not thought possible. We endured it, because such grief will either destroy you or strengthen you, and in enduring it, maybe we were strengthened.

But I know that somewhere in Bosnia there is a field soaked in blood and rotten with corpses, and that part of me is still there, and will be forever.

Colin Mackay
June 1998

Journey to a War

Crossing Over

Black morning, and I sit by the river
shaving in the light of our headlamps
and trying to ignore the tremble in my arm,
while the moon silvers the little waves
below the bridge.

All around me other men
are shaving, washing, filling kettles
– who cares if soap gets in the water?
And there is no bravado
because we are all too scared
for pompous words.
We know what we are in for.

Yesterday evening a group of children
tossed a bouquet of flowers
onto the water.
In my poor German I asked them
what they were doing.
"Praying for peace," they said.
They wore crucifixes,
carried pictures of Jesus and Mary,
and sang:
Lamb of God, have mercy on us.
Lamb of God, grant us peace.

And without their faith,
without a crucifix, a picture,
or even a flower,
I wanted to join them.

And there was the moonlight on the water,
so I raised my eyes to the source
and said out loud,
"Please don't let it all be for nothing."

Came the cry of an owl
over the river,
came the muffled talk of the border guards
on the bridge,
and the intimate sounds of sleeping men.

Now crossing into the troubled land
with the first red of the gloaming
just a hint beyond the dark mountains,
hungry war
stretches out its quivering fingers
to grip our throats,
and down on the road,
over the roof of the cabin
and into my heart

pours the moon.

The Office

It was in the office one day that I heard
old Joe from Accounts,
whom I had passed in the corridor often enough,
though hardly ever spoken to,
or met knocking back the juice at some retirement bash,
had a van which he wanted to take to Bosnia
because of the horrors he had seen on television,
and I said Yes, count me in.

Young Misha was a Russian student I met
at a party, standing forlornly in the corner
amid loud music and shrewd talk.
He made our eager third.

We raised money in the office – five hundred pounds –
filled Muriel up with carrier bags of medicine
and tins of supermarket food –
macaroni, corned beef, baked beans, that sort of thing –
and drove off down the A1.

Cockcrow

That evening there were shots in a far country,
shots, then a child
dead under a cherry tree.

I love to walk among trees,
I love when water runs under their branches,
the air sags over mossy rocks
and the burn is full of sunlight,
I love the way the branches lean over
and look at their reflections.

Now I look for a dead child
under a cherry tree.

That evening our dreams were pierced.
That evening we waited
till word came
winged like an angel
over the cities, over the plains,
over the silent seas.
Our resolution
was weak as flesh,
bounded by fading light.

And in his garage
Joe revved the engine,
and in his bedroom
Misha dug out the maps.
And in my garden
under the cherry tree
I heard the singing
that seemed to come from within the earth
and called us all
to the cockcrow we could not deny.

In Convoy

On we go.

The convoy is a mile long, and our van,
a Volkswagen, green, with the name *Muriel*
painted on the side (don't ask me why),
is the smallest vehicle in it.

Under the blue flag armoured cars
of the French Foreign Legion shepherd us forward.

The mountains approach from the distance,
their cry comes with the wind,
and like walls they enfold us,
like walls, and the strange land
falls still as a muted drum.

Passing Through

The city we pass through.
The streets are full of rush-hour traffic,
shoppers, plastic signs –
but sometimes we see farm carts
piled high with belongings.
Refugees,
people with haunted faces,
people from newsreels.
I stare, look away.
Their faces follow me.

We stop for a convoy
full of soldiers so young
they still get a kick out of shaving.
We pass flats with satellite dishes,
and children playing with toy guns
on the grass verge
who wave at us.

Wave and smile happily.

Political Rally in Zagreb

People sprout up like mushrooms in the park.
Baseball-caps, T-shirts, jeans, tracksuits –
any crowd, any where.

I am among Nazis,
There it is, the flag of the Movement,
and pictures of the late dictator,
a slab-jawed brute
once chided by Hitler for his cruelty.

And the afternoon sun dapples them all with gold,
the stern old veteran with medals on his chest,
and the young woman pushing babies in a pram.

Doglike, I hear notes beyond their range
and slink back into the shadows,
away from the pain of their unyielding love.

The Gabriel Hounds

Campfires in the night
where we sit and tell tales.

The stars of the high country
shine in their hundreds
and wild geese cry overhead.

Then a rumble in the distance
and the horizon prickles with flame.

War – right in front of us.

No one says anything.

The geese continue on their way
across the void.

Sometimes

On Serb television
the balladeers sing patriotic songs.
Serbia one!
Serbia free!
Serbia classless!

Sometimes
I think I could transfer my loyalties
to this fabulous Serbia,
land of the white eagle,
watcher by the gates of Europe,
because I am so heartily sick
of being pushed around and ordered to tolerate endlessly
the intolerant scumbag who pisses in my face
and shits on my parents' graves.

Sometimes, you see,
I am a patriot.
I long to belong
to a true national community
of hard-working cheerful people
who face the future with rolled-up sleeves,
stand when the anthem is played,
and don't snigger at the word "country".

Sometimes too I am a crusader,
like the boy of nine I used to be,
a little frayed around the edges now
but still ready to lead the charge
on the battlefield where Tsar Lazar* died
with all his cavalry.

Yes, sometimes I find,
in this disappointing place of ours,
that I have Serbia on my mind.

---

* Tsar Lazar: ruler of Serbia, killed fighting the Muslims at the battle of
Kosovo in 1389.

In Bosnia

The Bridge on the Sava

When we cross the river into Bosnia
we cross floating corpses.
They roll in the yellow water under the bridge
and grin up at us.
Their lips are drawn back from their teeth
and their bony fingers scuttle over the pebbles
like crabs.
They look hollow-eyed at the world above,
their ruined faces are
inexpressibly sad.

And I think of those comforting words
of the poet, that death
shall have no dominion,
and I realise how false they are,
for in this place death has dominion
over everything,
and we all await him,
supplicants at the door.

Do my eyes avoid yours, brother?
We shall none of us walk
along a riverbank again
without seeing the eyes,
and the grins,
and the scuttling crabs
there in the water.

When we cross the river into Bosnia
the sun is at its highest,
but our night has already come.

The First Day

Beside the dressing-station the dead
lie in neat rows, waiting for attendants
to zip them into body-bags.
They lie in a small suburban park
dotted with blue and yellow flowers,
in the shadow of tall poplar trees
with hearts and arrows carved on their bark.
They lie beneath a sky full of sunlight
in a cloud of flies,
and the breeze ripples the uncut grass
making the flowers dance
around the still grey faces.
It lifts the sweet smell
of blood, vegetation and meat-rot
and throws it at us.
Our convoy slows to a crawl
beside the gardener's hut where
a Red Cross flag is now hanging,
and we stare
at the corpses there in that neat pasture
where flies dance.

Up until now it has been fun.
A three day drive along the autobahns
with the country rising higher around us
till we were in a land of alps and cowbells.
And when we finally crossed the river it was on a morning
when the sun was crowning the mountains with glory,
and we were arsing around like children.
Our French commander came down the convoy
in his white UN jeep with a megaphone.
Attention! Attention! Ten minutes, we go!
A vos places, kids! We hit the road now, okay?
Dix minutes! Vite!

Steh auf! Weiter marschieren! shouted the Belgians.
Marchez, marchez! the Germans answered, laughing.
And the big lorries roared into life.
Joe was at the wheel, me on the left,
with young Misha sitting between us.

One for all! I said.
And all for one! they chorused.
We shook on it.
The Swiss in front and Norwegians behind
gave us victory signs.
Sarajevo, here we come!

But now across the river drifts the smoke of war,
now across that river comes the smell of blood,
across the corpse-laiden river echo the gunshots.
We peer at the world through bullet holes,
we who barely knew each other.
Suddenly we have no manly jokes
that would entertain the saloon bar,
we have no clever words.
We just stare at each other
and say
nothing.

Pigs

Morning sky
blue as the robe of glory
warm as my dreams.
What still lives in the meadow
settles on what doesn't.
The butchered grow a million
black buzzing wings.

In the burnt-out cafe
stray pigs from a nearby farm feed
on Ivan the chef and his two pretty waitresses.

Somewhere
the thud of mortars,
somewhere the splatter of shots,
the scream of an incoming shell,
but beyond the blackened hole
where the window used to be
under the still-functioning Coca-Cola sign
the pigs feed on.

And I gape at them,
I can't take my eyes off them.
Everyone else is appalled, but
I laugh
because it is so funny to see pigs
sitting in a cafe eating roast humans
that I laugh
and can't stop laughing
until a medic in a blue helmet
comes and sticks a needle full of something
into my arm and I fall asleep.

And dream of the morning sky
blue as the robe of glory,
warm as my childhood,
which stretches all the way back
to Scotland where
the office will be having its coffee break
about now and the Number 27 bus

will be halfway up Dundas Street
and no one will believe that
any of these things are happening
in the same world as the office
and the 27 bus.

Dreaming, they will say, dreaming,
you have cracked up, you
can't tell dream from reality
any more, and perhaps they are right –
certainly they are right.

But the pigs are still feeding
on Natasha's breasts and Ivan's buttocks
done to a nicety and crisp round the edges,
and the morning sky
is blue as the robe of glory
and warm as my love,
so glad to be alive
to make these ashes speak.

Incomprehension

We come over the hill in our big dusty lorries
expecting to be loved.

We bring food and medicine,
we promise to stamp out disease,
poverty, misery, hate and war.
We expect to be welcomed with open arms.
We are not.

People look at us askance.
In the corners of their eyes flickers
the red triangle of resentment.
We talk peace,
they nurse their guns.
We promise hope,
they spit sideways,
and when one of their women
blows a kiss at us,
they call her a whore.

Behind their doors they sing battlesongs,
plan the next campaign
and nourish their hate.

Mothers sew shirts for their boys
embroidered with magical symbols
to make the unbelievers' bullets bounce off.

I have seen boys, dead, in these shirts.
I have touched their blood.

Their blood is on my hands
when we leave in our big dusty lorries.

It will not wash off.

Civil War Requiem

Landscape of ashes.
All around, tortured soil
torn by tank tracks.
All around, rusty grass
stiff with blood.
By day, corpses dance
to the music of machine-guns.
At night, barbed-wire
plays the requiem of the icy wind.

Nights with no moon,
song under the red earth of Bosnia.

Landscape of torment
carved into the retina.
What is seen withers my tongue,
makes my gut sick
and heart despair.
A pregnant woman
has hanged herself on a tree.
The sky crashes around her,
the world screams.

Nights with no moon,
song under the red earth of Bosnia

Landscape of tears
trapped in the memory.
With every thought
a bit of my boyhood drowns.
With every thought
I am back over the burned hill
in that ashen land
where we buried them both,
their faces shrouded in pain.

Died Laughing

Rocket streaking overhead –
duck down fast
or you are dead.

Bomb tumbling through the air –
make sure you're
not standing there.

Bullets whizzing very fast –
enjoy that breath
could be your last.

Rocket, bomb and bullet play
turn your insides out today.

Knock you flat onto the ground,
toss your guts all around.

Tragic king becomes a clown,
big white face
and red-mouthed frown.

Silly head and ripped-up clothes,
goggle eyes
and squashed red nose.

Send him jumping through the hoop
with your metal in his croup.

Rocket, bomb and bullet say
we'll make a joke of you today.

Children's Hour

Look, the boy militia are playing
stalk-the-sniper in the street.
They are young, they are young as virgins,
one of them wears a Mickey Mouse T-shirt.
His toy rifle crackles.
A hundred yards away a brick
dissolves into dust.

In the evening it is raining.
One of the militia lies down beside me in the ruins.
The rain hits the metal sheet above our heads.
He is so young, his cheek is soft
and there are three notches on his gun.
"One for each Serb," he says.

And laughs. He laughs.
I cannot believe he is nourished on madness.
He doesn't shave, he has notches on his gun.
He is so young, young as a virgin,
and he laughs, this killer,
then blushes
and asks about girls.

So we talk in the rain,
we talk and talk till he is tired
and rubbing his nose with his fist.
Then he curls up and is soon gently snoring,
and Mickey Mouse plays with bullets in his head.

One day he will be man enough to kiss his girl,
this boy who has shot three men dead.

The Suicide Bomber

He thinks clouds.
Walking among the high windows
and communing with rooftops,
though he has streetlights for eyes
and his veins are gutters,
though his heart is a rubbish bin
and his head an engine
assembled with nuts and bolts –
clouds,
clouds he knows,
the beautiful clouds are his destiny.

The lord of the low-life has risen
so high he drifts in clouds
ablaze with dreams of glory.
Now he is master of the mountain.
On its peak he talks to the cosmos
while those below in darkness
wallow and die.

And on the day when the king of the vermin
shall whistle up his rats,
the child of the sky is ready
and willing
to climb the road to the stars.

Dead Silly

I was talking to a man who got shot dead.
A bullet hit him in the head.
Out of my mouth I picked his brain.
I don't think I'll eat meat again.

There were bits of him lying all around,
so I dug a hole in the ground
and put his skull inside his hat.
Then a tank came and squashed him flat.

He was so flat he couldn't get flatter.
All that was mind was now just matter,
and all his matter was turned to mush,
a long red streak across the dust.

I must admit it does still shake me
to see what a mess the body can become when guns and things start popping
and folk like you and me start dropping.

There is no dignity when you drop.
Everything goes kerflip kerflop.
You shit your pants and piss your leg.
Forget what you were 'cos now instead
you're just fertiliser for roses
and all your friends will hold their noses.

Bosnian Notebook

1
Who hurries the leaves of autumn
when they fall?
The mortar battery.

2
The sum of all our learning.
A blackboard
with bullet holes through it.

3
Daylight,
and the snipers come out
like birds.

4
We shave in the river.
Corpses float past us.
No one says anything.

5
The snipers make a truce.
Baywatch is on the telly.
They all have satellite.

6
A pretty woman
raped dozens of times
gives birth to a hand-grenade.

7
The militiaman was deeply religious.
Chastely he pushed his gun barrel up her vagina
and pulled the trigger.

8
A boy with bare feet.
Death has knocked him
out of his brand-new trainers.

9
A cup of corpse water
boiled to kill the bacteria
and a Typhoo teabag – Bliss!

10
Islamic volunteers.
Medieval knights
with machine-guns.

11
In Bosnia
the old man seizes me –
"Tell the world what is happening!"

12
In Britain
the suit yawns –
"Who wants more atrocity stories?"

13
Survivors of Srebrenica.
A woman offers me her daughter
for a dozen tins of corned beef.

14
Night,
and a sky machine-gunned
with stars.

15
I am shocked
because I am no longer shocked
by what I have seen.

16
I won't write these lines
for at least five years.
Madness otherwise.

The Germans

Horst and Anton from the Rhineland
weren't even born when the Wehrmacht
rampaged in these mountains.
Nor were their fathers.
That sin was in their grandfathers' day,
and their grandfathers were impressionable boys
who got conscripted.

Horst and Anton drive a great Opel
piled high with medical aid.
Old women parted with their pensions,
children handed over pocket money,
supermarket managers offered big discounts,
and a trade union branch bought them their lorry
so they could come here
and be at risk like this,
on a winding road littered with wrecks
and cartridge cases.

I am old enough to remember when
German meant bogeyman,
German was Nazi, jackboot, thug,
screaming bombs and barking orders.
I remember all that.
But now,
seeing Horst and Anton patiently dismantling the walls of pain
and pulling the slaughterhouse to pieces with their love,
I swear I will strangle the next hack
who makes a Kraut joke
in the pages of the Daily Cocksucker.

Everywhere there are children of the swastika,
but not these boys.
They are free of it.
Their Germany is clean.

For Johnny

One

We came to this place from many countries
in lorries and vans that snaked nose to tail
through the mountains.

Our red crosses made us look
like crusading knights, you said, laughing
as you lit your final cigarette ("forty
a day all my life and damn all the worse!").
So thoughtlessly you turned to the bullet
that levelled you.
It swung you in its arms
like a graceful dancer.

"Oh Christ!" you said
and died with your eyes open, face gone squint
and cigarette burning still on your lip
as the blood came.

But I expected more,
more blood, more high drama, more sensation.
I could not reconcile this with your end,
one red smear and the smell of your bowels
spilling over the Bosnian earth.

Why had nothing prepared me for the squalor
of this going?
I sat beside your husk
while night came with the throbbing of motors,
the distant rumble of artillery
and crackle of sniper fire in the woods.

Overhead the wild geese keened
the song of your abandonment.

Two

By the waters of the Neretva I sat down and wept
for you, Johnny –
you with your lopsided grin
and the fag dangling from your lip,
your hair going grey at the edges
and your crooked teeth,

your daft Liverpool supporter's scarf
and all your rotten knock-knock jokes,
your determination to get through
and your unlikely courage,
your hope,
and my hope,
in our job to be done.

Your hands reach into my silence.

Three

Filthy and weary of war
I squat on the darkening riverbank
and the shadowy Neretva reaches
out to me with her transparent fingers.
"Come," she says, and I step right into her
coolness and wade amongst the floating stars.

The rivers of Bosnia are brimming
with the tears of orphans; they are heavy
with the lamentations of widows.
The Drina and the Spreca, the Jadar
and the Bosna, the Unac, the Sava,
the angry Vrbas, and the Neretva
that unfolds herself like a battleflag
streaming through the mountains of Dalmatia.

Here they fought the Turks, the janissaries
of Suleiman the Magnificent; here
Tito led his partisans against the Third Reich.
They have been waiting for us a million years,
these rivers of peasants and heroes.

For six decades the Mersey flowed past you,
and I forget how many thousand times
I've crossed our own little Water of Leith.
Neither of us had ever heard of this Neretva
until a few weeks ago,
and she was just a blue line on a map.
Now we are both tied to it
with pliant threads.

Four

I have seen the militia of Mostar in their prime
ride down the cratered road towards some horror
that seemed familiar, safe almost,
because films had made it so.
I have seen them go,
all bandoleers, headbands and anxious grins,
old men swearing never to give in,
schoolboys dressed up like Rambo,
excited because girls had kissed their rifles and said
"Go kill our enemies, and God's."

All doubt was mine;
they did not hesitate to kill and die for Bosnia.
They erected walls of hate
between themselves and their Serb brothers
that nothing could break through.

One man there was, young
– you knew him, Johnny –
he had fuelled himself with fantasies of violence
rather than go with girls.
He could have been my son.
I saw him die.
A bullet blew his brains out.
They hit the wall.
"He died for Bosnia," they said.
"Allah is merciful."

Five

Oh, you knew the risks –
we knew them from the start –
that in this place of civil war
we would enter an impenetrable dark
where no red cross could save us
from the hate-filled heart
and the finger on the trigger.

You knew, damn it, it made sense,
one of us was bound to fall
sooner or later, the risks were just too great,
the odds so immense,
one of us had to go west.

But why you, Johnny,
why you of us all
to get a bullet in the chest?

You were the oldest by far.
"Vati", they called you.
"Der Alte". "The old man".
In another year you would have
your bus pass, carpet slippers,
and the fruits of your pension plan.

Death is so inappropriate for the peaceful.
You should be pottering in your garden,
seeing to your roses,
taking your grandchildren to the sea.
Instead, killed among bullets,
killed and decomposing,
and your face stares up at me.

Night comes,
the convoy murmurs,
and the cold rain swirls savagely.

Six

There are trenches on the hill, and rifle pits.
Below, a burned-out armoured car
raddled with splinters,
and a field of corpses that was once
a platoon of Serbian infantry.

Somewhere underneath it all,
trodden deeper with every passing year,
the mouths of other dead soldiers,
Owen, Rosenberg, Sassoon.

In Bosnia sorrow stands like a stork on one leg,
mutely brooding.

Seven

We had everything in that convoy.
Old Austrian Catholics who celebrated a wayside Latin mass
and young French atheists ripe from the Sorbonne.
There was love in abundance, love in all forms
from the middle-aged Russian with Rasputin eyes
who claimed to be the shaman of some tribe

in remotest Siberia,
to the two Spanish boys, less than half my age,
who were glued to each other,
held hands and kissed.
They looked so good the bullets spat.
And blond young Germans too,
peaceful as the moon.

We had everything there,
except guns, kevlar helmets, flak jackets,
or the ability to turn away bullets
by magic or by prayer.

Eight

In the morning which I have to face without you
daylight is weeping on the Neretva,
daylight is weeping but I am not,
daylight is weeping as our engines cough into life
on the battlefield of dreams.

The convoy must get through.

Nine

"Thank you, thank you," says the old woman of Sarajevo.
That is all her English.
Our convoy gives up its supplies –
corned beef, macaroni, baked beans,
packets of bandages, disinfectant –
this is what we have brought,
this is what my friend died for.
It will help other lives endure.

This is why she says, "Thank you, thank you,"
old woman with the twisted face,
her family dead in the war.
A burst pipe pumps raw sewage into the street.

"I had a friend," I say.
"Johnny was his name."
Somehow she knows.
She stands carefully up on her toes
and kisses me with lips like old leaves.
It is she who holds me
until my shoulders cease to shake.

Love in this Country

Love in this country
is not a matter of passion,
the high romance
that best-selling novels might be written about,
or adolescent sulks
made better with pop candy and counselling.

No, none of that.

Love in this country
is purely about survival,
and that is a matter of passion.

It is what a woman feels
seeing her man off to battle,
wanting him to win
and hoping he won't get killed doing it.

It is what a man thinks
when he crouches with his rifle
and prays that his home isn't in ruins
and his family lost or butchered.

And it is in a tin of food
a roll of bandages
a syringe of penicillin
a drink of water.

Anything.

Even in teaching that naked toddler
we found in the holocaust
how to wipe her own backside.

Incident

In the dark time
Mustafa Rodic, schoolteacher
from a small town in Bosnia,
was cycling home
with his bag full of geography essays
to be corrected,
when he ran into four paramilitaries
who didn't like his religion,
or his skin, or the colour of his eyes,
or some fucking thing,

so they tied him to a lamp post
with plastic wire,
hacked his genitals off
and stuffed them in his mouth.
Then they stood around laughing
while he bled to death.

Their footprints in the blood
made a new map.
Mustafa never taught it.
Perhaps that's why they killed him.

They took photographs of each other.
In the photographs
they are smiling boys,
they hold their knives like ice-cream cones
and their faces are unremarkable.

Only Mustafa is odd,
his mouth is rusty
and his eyes
are bugged with horror.

Tarik by the Roadside

We found you in the golden valley
when the day was bright without anxiety of rain
and no clouds scowled in the sky.
We found you beside the crucifying road
where the refugee column had passed
on a trail of dirt and tears.
The sun was at its highest
when we found you,
there, face down on the bitter tracks,
and suddenly the day lost its eyes
and was wormwood,
cold blood and ashes.

Tarik, we searched for the wounds that had killed you
and found too many.
Your eyes were swollen,
and your lips were bloody.
On your chest a tree of welts
flowered with midnight bruises.
Across your soft stomach
lay the path of the rifle-butt,
and your back bore the stigmata
of the lash.

As we turned you, Tarik,
your bones moved.
Your broken bones creaked and groaned
inside your sack of flesh.
We felt them shudder under our fingers,
the splintered ribs, the smashed foot,
your tortured skeleton protesting
as you no longer could,
and your blood slid out into the earth
singing of all your sorrows.

Oh Tarik, you had endured everything they did to you,
but inside you were dying!
Death had already kissed you
when you dressed yourself clumsily
and combed your black hair

with fingers that were cracked.
Death was already holding you
when you staggered through the door
of the torture chamber
into a sun too raw for you to bear.

Death was your good companion,
your one true friend.
He helped you on your way with kindness
when all else had abandoned you.
When everything and everyone was gone,
he alone held you,
wrapped in the green embrace of gangrene,
and comforted you
with icicles and frozen lilies,
with dreams of apples and the sad moon,
with coldness that numbed your pain.

Now your head lies on stony ground
and your dreams wander, deprived
of the once mysterious blood
and the warm sustenance of flesh.
They wander, Tarik, they wander back
to the day when you first loved a woman,
to the place where you played your childhood games
and the afternoon carried Time on her shoulders
and you looked at Creation, and
oh, it was so good!
Now death covers you with his soft ashes,
and you lie in the grey arms of the wind
beside a wretched road in Bosnia
surrounded by strangers who cannot find
the last word in your mouth
to open the gates of the morning
and set the stars on fire.

So you left us, Tarik.
So the shadows came,
and whatever hope for the future you had
fled before them
like a cloud before the wind.
You took passage,

for in the midst of that torn land
peace has her secret passageways
winding through the violent dawns
and withered dusks of a century
grown weary with walking the earth.

You left us, Tarik,
you took the road
through towns emptied of song,
and the shade and silence of forgotten forests
where wounded men crawl to die after battle.
You left us,
and we three, resting on our one spade,
looking at the job that had to be done,
felt a deep sadness for you,
passage of impossible dreams,
the sadness of love.

We buried you there.
This hole we dug with our fingers
and our one spade.
This our Christian hands achieved
in your Muslim earth.
This grave by the sombre roadside
in the meadow of sorrow.

And there we laid you, Tarik,
we three fools
in the shadow of our tears.

The Sheltering Sky

Before the racket of killing began again
there was a moment of great calm
when kneeling by the grave we had scraped
for that poor bastard on the roadside
I felt God's hands stretch down to us,
gently lift our chins, and there
was the sudden inexplicable fact
of the blue sky which stretched all the way home
above a landscape saddened with ruins,
and on it one bird hung immobile in heraldic grandeur,
where the smoke ended.

My companions asked me to say something
over the dead man, and I did so,
but not as a Christian,
because he was one on whose face
Christians had hacked the Son's gallows
with the point of a knife,
and I could not beg forgiveness for them,
for I had no right to forgive,
or wish to.

So I hung back,
and there in the darkness behind mumbled words
my eyes sought those solitary wings,
so fierce and so untamed,
the moment they swooped to fish
in the sea of grass.

That evening a church bell rang far up the valley,
irrigating dried-up consciences
and calling the militia to arms.
We saw them go,
boys and old men swinging past the tower
with rifles on their backs,
turning its simple cross
into the shape of their desire.

We heard them singing,
then the sun went down.

Convoy at Night

Night in the mountains,
the one road gone lunar with shell holes,
and we sleep beside our lorries.
Huge Volvos and Renaults loom over us
like cathedrals, and our van
our little church
a shadow in the shadows.

And the night is petrol-stained.
We wrap diesel around us,
we wrap the smells of supper,
birchwood fires
and soft mother earth.
We wrap starlight and snores,
the haze of instant latrines
and hot tyres and dreams stolen
from countries that are not at war.
Comes the sounds of the night birds
which I am too much of a city boy to identify,
the little crackings and rustlings in the dark,
the slow, careful steps of the sentries.

They say there are bears in these mountains,
they say there are wolves.
I know there are snipers
and will happily take my chances
with bears and wolves and anything else
that isn't carrying a high-velocity rifle.
I am afraid.
Who is here beside me?
The shadow of a gunman,
the shadow of a bomb,
the shadow of my own body
broken to pieces in a hospital bed.
And the syllables die,
and the words crumble in my mouth,
and in the shadows only
fear
remains.

Cleansing

In the High Planina

Above the broken road
the stallion country rears up.
Dark mountain peaks are its hooves,
capped with a mane of billowing clouds.
Gleaming flanks of cliff fall sheer
hundreds of feet into valleys
where streams clatter over black rocks.

Javor*, say the sons of this earth,
Treskavika, Majevica Planina.
Cruel, grand is the place that we find
out there beyond our windscreens
where the war crouches.

When night walks in,
and the sky is lit with stars,
we listen for the roar of the battleground
and the steps of the dead walking
in the place of ashes.

When day wanders over the forest
we look for the word in its mouth,
and it is terrible
with a beauty like tears.

**Javor, Treskavika, Majevica – the principal mountain ranges (planina) of Bosnia.*

Serbian Church Near Zvornik

High, the onion domes
topped with silent swords.
High, the roof of fire.
The walls drop down to trodden earth,
the smell of rotting wood,
sweet and old,
where rain eats through the rafters
and worries the floor of the crypt.

The air is rich with incense.
Old men in golden robes
enact the mystery,
feed the famished cry
with bitter bread.
Young fighters ask God to bless
their machine-guns,
and outside in the weeping air
their song resounds,
and the smell of decay rises
above the domes' golden cry
and the slaughter-bird's nest
to greet the Muslims
whose graves are in
the clouds.

In the Graveyard

The rain falls like the tears of Jesus.
It rivers down the windscreen
and the wipers kick their legs in the air,
it rattles over our heads like a tap-dancer,
it sizzles under our tyres.
It falls on the wretched people on the road,
it falls on the soldiers in the mountains,
and on their graves,
it falls on our hearts.

The road forks at a bridge,
but only half the bridge is there,
half of it is in the river.
There is a village on the other side where no dog barks.
On this side is a graveyard and a roofless church.
There are tank tracks across the graveyard
and the tombs are tumbled and smothered with weeds.
Ancient corpses, excavated by artillery, lie in bits and pieces.
Two recent dead are swollen and rotting
and wear their smell like a danger sign.
The rain fills the suppurated flesh of the child
and the mouldy eye-sockets of his ancestor's skull.
Bones gleam like old silver in the downpour.
Green stones, old as ages.

Inside the church are the burial vaults of Imperial Austria,
the Bosniaks of Prince Eugene,
the dreaded red-cloaks of Marshal Daun,
and the loyal frontier guard of white-whiskered Franz Josef.
They lie amidst carved death's heads, crossed sabres,
panoplies of flags, and names of forgotten battles.

Around the ruined graves are inscriptions by today's fighters.
*I hope I don't get killed, but if I do please give my stamp
collection to my sister.*
*The invincible third battalion can take on anything except
Josip's cooking.*
Now or in a hundred years we shall win.
Mico loves Nikolina.
I wish I wasn't here.
Help.

And above the broken altar what is left of the crucifix
hangs under the weeping sky.

The Opening of a Mass Grave
Near Srebrenica

In the blue autumn
images of smoke and flame
adorn this desolate place.
Where terror once strode fearlessly
under the eyes of the butcher
there is now only dread.

In the blue autumn,
though the hour of the shootings is behind us
and the voice of the screaming
is still, and birds sing again,
dread comes tap-tap-tapping
his blind man's stick.

No one weeps in the blue autumn
because the dead have no tears.
When they tore open the last secret passages
our joy followed their blood
into the ground.

Now in the blue autumn
it is cold, so very cold,
and dread enters in
with the eyes of a beast –
tap-tap
tap-tap
tap . . .

The Cleansing

They come before dawn,
noisily, they know the way.
They know the steps to the house,
and they know every house,
every door where the damned dirt lives.
They have them marked down,
carefully documented, they are
thorough, they make no mistakes
in the act of cleansing.

The sanitation trucks rumble through the streets.
Come to us, you dirt, come and be washed,
damned dirt, come over the hill.

Columns trudge over the hill,
all young men, all boys,
and the women weep, the girls
stretch out their arms and cry,
but the columns trudge on over the hill
to the hoses of the sanitation department
that wash them with bullets.

Town, little town
of cuckoo-clock houses,
white walls and red roofs dressed with flowers,
town, you are clean now,
the dirt is gone.
Come out, laugh, dance and be saved!

Silence.

Town, your air is musty with cleanliness,
it has the hush of fading echoes.
I shall walk your wooden streets
in the red executioners' light.
I shall walk with your houses,
your empty houses from which they swept
the men who played football
and the boys who liked girls.

We shall all walk over the hill
to where your damned dirt lies now,
town, little town, empty town,
fertilising the meadow grass,
their backs bedecked with roses.

The Flies

That's how we find it, empty.
In the street are two or three cars
with their tyres shot to ribbons,
and a can the breeze is playing with.

Here no one comes.
The grocer's shop, the pub, the video rental,
hang lopsided, their windows on the pavement,
footprints in the glass smashed to sand,
and the remnants of looting.

No blood, no bodies,
even the dead have forsaken this place.
By the door of the mosque
one cartridge case.

Then suddenly we hear laughter
and pause, look at each other unhappily.
Who is laughing in this eerie place,
and why?

Danger!
But it attracts us, yes it does.
Like moths we flutter along the wall
to the laughing flame.
A house, closed but not locked.
We go in –

and as we enter
the TV roars with laughter.
A German quiz game dubbed into Serbo-Croat.
Prizes bob past, and a beautiful hostess
in a shimmering gown grins insanely.

Food spilled on the table,
a jam pot open and crawling with flies,
butter black with them.
Where have they all come from?
Dead flies lie on the windowsill.
Live flies watch television
and feed.

Posters of rock stars, footballers
and pin-ups buzz past.
The flies eat pizza, they stagger to the jam
and draw tracks in the butter,
they shit and lay their eggs everywhere.

Buzz buzz they go like a disco night,
buzz buzz like a shopping mall,
like a war zone, buzz buzz.

We leave it as we found it.
The TV raves
and flies throw themselves at the bloody glass.
They die there.

By the Riverside

After the battle,
as the day scatters its murmurs of angry flame,
a girl strips by the riverside
and shakes her hair over the water,
while the tide caresses her soft body
and sings.

And I think that she is so lovely
just for being alive,
with the sun and moon for breasts
and rainbows for thighs.

She rises
and dries her long brown limbs,
ties her hair in a tight band,
pulls on her jeans,
buttons up her blouse,
and takes her rifle in her hand.

And I watch her hips
swing like chiming bells,
causing the feeding crows to start.
And she is lovely
for being alive –
but death is in her heart.

Bosnian Elegy

The day came up with darkness.
Fires paled, but smoke hung over the ruins,
and out of the smoke came things
we had wanted to forget.

The dead lay in their wet shadows.
There were so many.
Under the bridge where the broken tree had fallen
they lay tangled in its branches,
a dam of rotting flesh,
and the water swelled around them,
swelled until the stream burst its banks
and flooded the path
where the cattle had gone, breathing gently,
in the days of long ago,
and the pastureland sprinkled with cowpats,
and the football pitch with the old broken goalposts,
and the lovers' bushes warm with passion.

The water followed them all,
drowning their tracks in the cold green,
and only our staring eyes were dry.

When we came away from that place
we walked unsteadily
with creaking limbs,
the shiver of ice water in our veins,
and the silence we could never forget.

Bosnia
over your pretty villages
the smoke hangs now.
Your white walls are hacked with bullets
and stained with blood.
We have seen your children dancing in the flames,
your men festooned with bullets and hand-grenades,
and your women raped by the dozen.

We shut our doors
because we did not want to hear the weeping.
We shut our ears, our hearts, our minds
because we did not want to hear the weeping.
But the weeping seeped through
like rainwater, like the clouds' tears,
like the grief of heaven,
and soon nothing could be heard
but the weeping.

Now, Bosnia,
your silence is my life.
Your grief pursues me
and I see your blood
dripping from the mournful sky.
Every day I see the smoke of your many burnings.
When the sun goes down
your passion wears a crown of flames.

The Burn

Evening. When we reached the hillside
the sun slid away from us like a thief.
Evening. We crawled over the skyline
on our stomachs so the snipers wouldn't see us.
That evening we heard the burn,
and we climbed onto a big boulder covered in moss,
and there was the water beneath us,
stitching down the glen in the nightfall,
and the moon came out,
and the hills stood like gravestones
deserted by their dead.

And when the darkness spoke
it was with the voice of an owl,
with the feet of a fox,
with the stealthy sounds of bracken
and the dance of the trees as the wind rose.

In our glen there was eternity,
but we could not forget the war
because we stank of war.
So we lay in the burn and let the water clean us,
let it wash the filth away to the waiting rivers,
to the Drina, to the Danube, to the distant Black Sea,
let it cradle us in its arms
soft as feathers, cold as death's honey-flow,
and we were a piece of it,
and at peace, and the war
was far away.

And the fox circled by the waterside
sniffing our scent,
and the eerie cry of the owl
hung on the wavering branches.
And fire stood in the distance,
and we heard its bloody rumble
once more.

Wild Geese

Whose cry is on the night wind
above the wall of damp firs
where the road from the west
soars into the mountains.
There the river lives, carving
its name through granite,
and the thick breath of the forest rises
like smoke into rafters of cloud.

We leave our hidden camp
and stand out in the open
on a spur of soft earth
heavy with the scent of sheep
and the sound of water falling
over white pebbles.

Oh, those fires on the distant plain,
those fires in the town we left
with the morning!
We stand silent
watching the deaths of many,
and we have no words, none,
our hearts, our hands, are desolate.

Comes
the cry
of the wild geese
bright with angry love,
and the beating of their wings
across the night.

Peace Talks

They say news has come through about negotiations
in some nice neutral place
with good catering
and lots of policemen.

They say there will be
meaningful talks,
a cease-fire resolution,
an end to the killings,
mass expulsions,
terror, intimidation
and rapings.

They say the inhumanity
must cease.
They say if it doesn't
they will bomb everybody to buggery
just like they did those rag-heads in Iraq.

They say they have been
very patient.

They say
and they say
and they say.

Question with Two Answers

In Bosnia I often thought
which is further away
the moon or Scotland?
Easy.
I'd met people who came from Scotland,
but I'd never met anyone who came from the moon.

In Bosnia I often thought
which is further away
the moon or Scotland?
Even easier.
At night I could see the moon,
I couldn't see Scotland.

Night Over Bosnia

Night.
And finally the world is at peace.
The sniper on the rooftop rests his rifle,
and because it is night
the artillery does not fire,
and even the mad dogs are in their kennels.

This is the hour of stealth and silence.
We pad through the rain
and pray we don't step on landmines.
We slink through the shadows
and pray to be out of this slaughter house
by daybreak.

Night
when even the Ustashas and Chetniks* must sleep
under the eternally incurious stars.

And somewhere in the Adriatic the American navy
prepares to throw its missiles at us.

*Ustashas, Chetniks - Croat and Serbian nationalist militias respectively.

Night Wind

Cries over the grassland
bring dusk
and the long empty hours.

Cold,
and we lie in our sleeping bags
under the moon
that many will not see again.

Song of a late bird
embraced by the darkness,
song of the wind
through the van's shattered door
open like an angry mouth,
song of the bullet hole.

Three men pretend to sleep,
three men caring for each other.
Our thoughts
lie unspoken beside us.
Our fears
cry on the wind.

The Village

Gethsemane

Village which I saw for the first time
when day hung webs of light over your ancient branches
and the river was a chuckle in copper-coloured distance.
Then the forest's throat was full of birdsong,
then the memory of patient ancestors
towered aloft where blackbirds nested
in a circle of whirring wings.

Then was harmony, purpose,
but should a redeemer be born in you today,
village no longer on the map,
what manger would shelter him,
what wise men would come
to this grave without a stone
where a hard-working people lie forgotten?

Village, dear village
the hour that has no stars
climbs over the black ditch
and the stones mark nothing but the passage of bullets,
and when the scars have all filled with moss
the lives of those who bled
will have been forgotten.

Village, let me never forget.
Live in my heart,
live in my soul and in my mind,
live through me
by me, in me
with me
let me be your life, your extinguished life,
let my words roll away ignorance
and open the nameless graves
so I may see your people walk forth again
as in the dawn, before the bullets came.

Village
which I saw for the first time
when love wrapped your branches
in layers of incandescent flame.

Svetlana in the Darkness

When the sun comes out
she unlocks the door and sighs
over the tormented earth.
When the moon comes out
she throws open the window
and sings to the stars.

Svetlana has found her voice
in a drop of water.
When the rain lashes the river
she sings anthems to the black grass.

She has made her beautiful body
out of midnight apples in the dark wood.
When the men trail back
dripping tears of blood
she comforts them with leaves,
she bathes them with water lilies,
and icicles spill over her warm heart.

Svetlana works by the light of a green lamp.
Through her eyes swagger pirates,
and her lips curl like the waves of a green sea.
Her fingers shield rotting wounds
and death stands in the doorway.

Svetlana, the boys cry,
your breasts are two islands in the infinite!
Svetlana, suckle me with your gentle fingers,
let me lose myself in your green ocean!
Death is staring in the window,
he is scratching the glass
with his long nails,
Svetlana!

And Svetlana in the darkness
sighs with the red crescent moon,
she sings the song of the sad earth.

Death listens from the doorway,
and the boys sleep in beds of water lilies,
sleep in boats of leaves,
sleep green, so greenly sleep,
until in an ocean of apples
they drown.

Days and Nights in the Valley

Your day, Svetlana,
walked up the valley in golden shoes,
and the sun that raised himself
from the land beyond the forest
and across the mountains of that other planet
over the river,
saw us there, two fond lovers
with hair full of freshly cut grass
in a meadow that was young
and lovely as the newborn hour;
and the rain that had danced for us
on the track the cattle took
was still, and still was
the murmur of the sleeping village,
and the hill's whisper arising
from the city of branches.

The old militiaman guarding the mosque
cried to the waiting wind –
Allah il ilallah!
The minaret bannered the smell
of beasts' breath and moist straw
in the air of the crying time
and the blue death, and the desert of light;
and we stretched ourselves on the earth
Svetlana, we stretched ourselves
in the comfort of our wounds;
for life was our red apple
cruelly cut in two,
and my weaker half cried to you, Svetlana,
shield me, shield me
between your serene breasts,
with the calm of your woman's strength,
with the calm of your river
and your village, and its ancient hearth
when day explodes around us
in all the plains of the sun.

Your night, Svetlana,
was a song of pine and water
and gently stirring bracken
as the valley slid off to sleep in the owl light.
Then earth's sister moon swam over us
while stars glinted like fishes in the depths above
and flowers closed their mouths on the deed
as night's breezes came and stroked our naked skin.

Around us we heard the world moving
through the turn of the forest's blood
in the realm of foxes, badgers and the hunting owl
who swooped from his icy nest
laiden with blades, and left
a small scream there on the trail of tears.

So we lay, Svetlana, we lay so
full of each other that we had forgotten war
and killing, and corpses floating in the river;
and out of our foolish hopes
a bright young star rose and soared
up the burning side of old heaven
and shone there, delirious with peace.

But beyond the trees, across the water
drunken Chetniks were cargoing into lorries
heavy with hate-loaded rifles,
and already they had made your soft throat
a necklace of bullets, already
they had opened you with their knives,
already they had nailed you down on the meadow
and made your womb a garland of guns.
Oh, sleep now, darling, nothing remains,
what was unique is gone forever;
your day searches the fallen sky
and cannot find you,
nor night in those mountains of the moon.

Bosnian Village

By the banks of the Drina
the pale village floats beneath the moon
and the muddy river turns its pebbles
into treasure.

At night the workfield is hidden.
The smell of it sinks back into the old wood,
and along the stony path
come the village heifers
in a heavy scent of byres and warm straw.

At night, only the owl hunts
in the moon-way,
in the time of small screams.
Night is soft with forgetfulness.

Tomorrow boys will fish corpses from the stream.

Tales

I told you tales, oh such tales I told you
about my home your eyes had never seen,
but where your heart had lived long in a place of solace,
and grand heather-covered mountains
and bagpipes crying through the mist.

Love told me these tales of a Scotland that never was,
and you listened wide-eyed
and believing each lie I told you.

Oh, sweet were these tales of mine!
And hate was distant, and war averted,
and in your arms I lay that night
with all my sweet lies beside me
wedding us together till the morning came.

And I left that day, and the coming night
kept me from your village and my death.
I left you with those of your people
deep in the green wood of the land of story,
deep in the place where love sits on a throne of stars.
I left you full of hope, I left you!
And in this world I never saw you more.

You Mock Us

You mock us with the beauties of the world.
You mock us with the summer sky,
the contented glow of evening
and dusty moonlight on softened city streets.
You mock us.
Even with love you mock, even with joy,
the ecstasy of cock and cunt
and the spurt of semen through the vagina's silken opening,
with the pant of animal fucking in hot youth
and the long cooling solitude of age,
even with those you mock us.

What I saw that day in the place of horror,
on the field that was so beautiful,
was murdered old men and children laid out in rows,
women raped, sprawled, mutilated in puddles of rotting matter,
and the one who was to have been my wife,
whom I loved more than Jesus and my own soul,
had a butcher's knife driven hilt-deep into her crotch,
and her pussy was black clotted with blood
beneath a bright blue sky that shrieked
mindless hymns to the beauty of your creation.
And I hated myself for believing you,
hated myself for trusting in your goodness.

Tell me, lord of promises,
has my Svetlana been reassembled in paradise?
Will I meet her there again one day?
Was the nine-inch blade I pulled out of her with a long dirty suck
just one more instance of your unknowable will?
Tell me, father of heaven, tell me, daddy,
don't turn your back on your sadface son,
don't be deaf to my questions,
roll this stone away,
resurrect my faith,
help me climb out of this pit of filth
and let there be a truce between my disgust
and the grandeur of your creation
so that I may yet learn how to praise your mercy
and regain the path that leads to the place
where all sorrows are forgotten.

I Would Call her my Girlfriend

but they tell me the word is patronising,
and it's true she was in her thirties
with two young children
and she turned old so quickly.

When I found her with the rest of her village
she was older than my grandmother
and just as dead due to the butcher knife
sticking in her vagina.

And then there was her daughter
whom I had carried on my shoulders that morning,
she was old too, like a great aunt,
and shrivelled with bullets.

Then the son – God knows where he is,
probably in a hole somewhere dug for a dead fighter,
because he was old enough to be a fighter
being about ten, and there were fighters

that age in Bosnia, plenty of them.
So they're quite right, I shouldn't patronise
and call her my girlfriend
because she was too old

old as death. Even her little daughter
was older than me when I dragged them both
to the ditch where all the others were laid out
and kicked earth over them.

Always

Ludmilla
how many times did we walk through the sunflowers
and you were skipping and war was a constellation away
and you were angelic and half way through my dull life I was
gushing sentimental over the kid I'd never had
and fitting myself out for the job of being a father?

I'd have made a good father, you know.
At least, I'd have tried.

I'd come through the border without a passport
smuggling ten thousand thoughts just to please you,
just so you could take them and play with them
and make toys out of them on the road of your smile
that had no ending, that ran on forever.

And when orange dusk fell on the world
Ludmilla
when the sun had passed from the battlefields of the east
right over our heads without killing us and gone down
somewhere near the battlefields of the west
where the smoke was rising
I sat with your mother and listened as she told you stories
about Prince Marko* and his magical horse
that could soar through the air like a jet fighter
made of warm godflesh and blood
without any bombs on board
strafing the hills with courage,
torching the ground with mystery.

Always
Ludmilla
I'll measure your face as it was just six years old,
I'll see your eyes brown as your mother's,
your freckles, your snub nose,
your surprising yellow hair all yours,
always
you'll be in your white ballet dress with pink shoes and
ribbons curled up against my chest
and I'll feel the delicate breath rustle in your nostrils

and whisper words of comfort to you
as I did that last day
when I held your head in my arms,
but there was no head there
just a mess of clotted blood, brain and insects
a red hole
and burnt hair.

Prince Marko: hero of Serbian legend.

The Grey Wind

And so the world ends,
but I am left to live on.

The wind runs over the roof of my ruin
and scratches at the window,
it gropes its way down the chimney
and I hear it there behind the bricks
moaning and weeping within inches of my head.
It's your name I'm trying to hear,
your name, Svetlana,
because only that will stop
my eyes filling with darkness.

But then the rain walks in hissing,
and the grey wind spits
the cold fact of destruction.

The Wanderer

Blue,
the road home.

Above the cordite stink,
above the screaming,
above the smoke and the echoes,
is the road through the air,
the road of my wish –
God, get me out of this place! –
the road that leads
round the curve of the world
home to Scotland
where no one will believe
the things I have seen,
the things which I cannot
believe.

Bosnia's dead walk before me,
Serb, Croat and Muslim,
as though it didn't matter,
reddening the meadow,
staining the white walls
with flecks of blood,
they ascend the way to the land of peace,
where silence waits for us all,
as it was in the beginning,
and no one knows what
a gun is.

The road home.
Blue.

Cold Night Lullaby

Cold night wind lashing the seawall.
My lover was gentle, her voice never raised.

Garden green as the fair hills of Bosnia.
My lover was fair as the fresh summer sky.

Black door opening on a desolate house.
My lover was butchered in a field of flowers.

Rain washing the road, sizzling in streetlight.
If I could cry for her my tears would never end.

Cry of a child, heartbeat of the world.
My heart lies beside her in a ditch of dead.

My lover waited for me one evil morning.
Now I wait for her and she never returns.

Finding Peace

Lot

You ask me what I did.
Survived.
That is all.

Part of me came back,
the part that is bone and flesh
and wants to eat and drink and live –
that part survived.

The other –
the other couldn't forget.
The other looked back,
and was turned into a pillar of salt.

Now I survive
without my other.

Now I hug that great absence
where love used to be,
and christen its pain
with the storm of my flesh,
with words.

Heartbroken River

Every night in Bosnia I asked,
let it pass from me
this cup of bitterness
brimming with the tears of widows,
with the grief of orphans
and with men's cruelty,
let it pass with the gunshots
and dissolve into the nothingness
that follows annihilation.

So many died there,
yet I survived.
So many went down in filth
while not a bullet scratched me,
no, not one,
even when I wandered gawking
across the murder field
that every one lay on,
puddling into the earth.
Even then
the cup would not pass.

Now tonight this same moon
shines on Bosnia too,
where the heartbroken river washes
the graves that we dug,
and the dead float to me
like leaves on the water,
they lean towards me
like grass before the wind,
and they point at me,
they point.

Every night that river
screams
in the moonlight.

Fear

Nothing had prepared me for it.
Nothing.

I had hoped my fear would be great,
terrible, metaphysical.
Instead it was squalid.

It was about windows, roofs,
piles of rubbish,
places from which a sniper's bullet
might come,
and would I be killed
or merely crippled,
and which would be
better?

I had hoped fear would purify me
of selfishness,
but it didn't.
Instead I prayed for the bullets
to go elsewhere,
kill and cripple other people,
but leave me alone.

And that's what happened.
Other people got killed and crippled
while I
wet
myself.

I don't know why I'm writing this now.
It doesn't make me any better,
or any braver,
or them
any less dead.

The Man with the Umbrella

When I came back
I had to relearn language.
This is a lorry,
it is not a tank.
That is a paving stone,
it is not a landmine.
There is an umbrella,
it is not a rifle.
The man who is carrying the umbrella
is not going to shoot me with it.
The man who is carrying the umbrella
is not going to shoot anyone.
I have no reason to fear
the man carrying the umbrella.

And when the man puts his hand
inside his jacket
he pulls out a radio,
not a hand grenade.
And when he switches the radio on
he is not detonating
a remote controlled device,
he is listening to music –
but the tune he is listening to
is the tune the militia listened to
when they machine-gunned their prisoners
against the wall I was
hiding behind.

And suddenly I see him,
I see his cruel eyes,
I see his rifle.

And I see the blood
on my own hands.

Blood of the Lamb

Remember
when we crossed the river children
were tossing flowers on the water
and praying for peace.

Lamb of God.

When we crossed the river my friend
was still alive and I thought
that he would live for ever.

You take away the sins of the world.

When we crossed the river I had
forgotten what woman is like,
how soft she can be, how kind.

Have mercy on us.

When we crossed the river I thought
there was a limit to human evil.
I thought that, you know, I really did.

Give us peace.

Now, as I trudge back across that damned river,
carrying the guilt of my survival
like a cross that crushes my shoulders,
the God I cannot pray to
gives me no peace at all.

To what am I returning? I ask.
To what, and is it worthwhile?
Can it be, with me in it?
The cross of my guilt crushes me
down into my footprints,
and – *look* – they are bloody.

Silent Voices

Silent voices
and me at forty-six
wondering who will love me now
that the only woman I ever loved enough
to want to see her, hear her, touch her
every day for the rest of my life
is dead and rotting in an anti-tank ditch
dug through a field in Bosnia.
Whose love will I be worthy of now,
who will take the time to wonder,
I ask the silent voices
that move through my still dim house
after the Off button has been pressed
and the smell of hot valves hangs there
like my useless thoughts waiting
for oblivion to happen.

I should tear up everything
and just sing a song about failure
having failed to do so many things
like save a single life that I know of
with all my good intentions,
or commemorate a single one of those who died
in such a way that the world would discard its weapons,
or write the great poem, novel, whatever
that would make her name immortal
like Dante's Beatrice,
or even catch the bullet that killed her in my chest,
even that I failed to do, even that.

So now I talk to the silent voices
and ask their forgiveness for being here,
for having survived for no reason,
for having come back to inanity,
for not being there with her,
for not being there,
for not having learned how to die.

Don't Ask

Don't ask me.
Don't ask me what I saw over there.
I don't want to talk about it.

I envied the birds
because they could fly away.
I envied the worms
because they weren't human.

I wished I could crawl out
of my skin and become
something else.

The apples were nice.
They grow nice apples there
There was a big tree
with juicy red apples
hanging from it.

Don't ask me what else
was hanging from it,
dripping.

The flies rose into the air
like the hair of the horror-stricken.

Don't ask me why.
I won't talk about it.
Leave me alone.

The Dead

At night they come to me,
the dead I have known,
the carbonated militiamen,
the girl with a bullet in her head.
They stand there in the darkness.
They have not forgotten.
They stand and stare at me,
the survivor.

They stare.

George

Out of the dinner party George comes yapping
that giving food to starvation victims is patronising,
that getting involved in a civil war is imperialism,
that pity is a bourgeois vice and very disreputable,
that raising money for charity is right-wing
and typical of the sort of thing that Hitler got up to,
not to mention Margaret Thatcher, Attila the Hun,
Rupert Bear, and Christ knows who else.

George
George
George
has always had plenty to eat,
never heard a gun go pop,
and lives well with money to burn.
I look at his foolish, grinning face,
remember the thin dead bodies rotting beside the Drina,
and try hard not to hate him.

I do not succeed.

Poor Ghost

When I came home from the war
people patted me on the head
like a good dog.

When I spoke
they were silent,
gave a good imitation of listening,
and stifled their yawns.

When I tried to explain
they nodded wisely
and thought I was exaggerating.

When I wept
they exchanged knowing looks.

And then they left
because
the next episode of the soap opera
was waiting for them,
and the National Lottery ticket,
and Pop Piddle's new CD.

They left
because
they would rather interact
with a computer game
or a TV screen,
and besides
I embarrassed them.

But really they left
because
I had died back there
and they didn't believe
in my ghost.

Exile

Under an alien sky, noise of evening in the city.
Offices exhale, a million people feed,
and fat clouds of sound encircle the tower blocks.
Under an alien sky lies this desert of windows.
Its solitude chatters with television.

Once our fathers' home was a place of joy,
the rustle of leaves on the edge of life
dappled with green sunlight
where children went, breathing softly,
into the summer's night.
Once we saw the morning in lilac time,
and as the blue deepened into autumn
the doors opened, and there stood our fathers
with outstretched arms, saying
Welcome, come to the table.
And we rested easy by the laughing fire
while the future sped towards us
like a shadow before the wind.

Now our fathers' home stands grieving in the rain and mist.
A corpse floats by on the black river
waving his arms.
Come, come, he wails,
mouth blubbering raw, face fish belly white,
eyes of silver.
Come, come, he wails,
and his thin arms clamber up over the jetty,
head rolling on his hollow shoulders,
and his tongue falls out.

Our cries lay in tatters
on the road where they killed the children,
our tears lost their way
in the sluggish flood of the Drina,
and our eyes swam westward,
away from the bloody wall
and the gunmen on the bridge
who guarded the darkness
so no one could steal it.

Tonight we hunger for the past,
we hear the sad music
that wrenched us from the blue.
Tonight in this soft land
our blood pulls us to that other shore,
and to the time of pain.
This is not our fathers' home, we say,
this place that shelters us with indifference.

Tonight we wander under an alien sky,
and our hearts are full of pain.
There are no friends,
no enemies,
no music,
no understanding,
no thoughts, hopes or desires.
Where such pain is
there is room for nothing else.

Hope and Prayer

Now
returning
to Scotland,
returning to the place
where there is no blood
in the gutter, returning to
this town, to this same street of mine,
to unbelievable ignorance or innocence
– O God, the things they don't know! –
returning to the office, returning to my colleagues,
to my neighbours, the daily shopping, and the quarrels
in the corridors, the gossip in the canteen and the pub yapping
about football, TV and football, pop music and football, lotteries
and football, football, football, returning to all this
– O God, the things they don't know! –
and finding these longed-for-streets so foolish,
so cold and empty, finding this life
a place of dross and echoes,
pray now, God of silence,
purify my heart,
God of water,
clean my
soul

for I have seen the dead
and bits of the dead, floating on the water,
and I pray,
God of night,
that you will grant me peace
my heart be cleansed, and my memories
be silent within me, even as the stars
are silent
now
and forever.

Earth and the River

That's all it takes.
I may be walking along a street or
working at my desk, when suddenly
the smell of wet earth or the sound of running water
comes out of nowhere, and I am back
there in the village by the Drina
stroking your dark hair,
listening to the gentle murmur
of your voice, while the rain drifts in
like gunsmoke over the meadow.

Then birds sang in the row of chestnut trees beside the path,
and farmers drove their cows down
out of the high fields to the low meadow pasture,
walking slowly behind their swishing tails
in the rich haze of cattle-breath and moist dung.

That's all it takes to see
Ahmad riding on the back of his heifer,
thin scrapped knees dug into massive flanks,
shooing the flies away with the baseball cap
that he always would wear sideways,
while Ludmilla skips along the path in front of him
dancing on the heels of her shadow
six years long.

When dusk came
we walked along that path by the river
as the moonlight rolled its silver ribbons
over waves and lichen-covered rocks,
and a solemn heron took flight towards the Serbian shore
where silent guns waited.

There, along the riverside
where your village had once sacrificed to the grain deities,
there, where Prince Marko
once fought your nation's oppressors,
there we talked nonsense, Svetlana,
in the old fort under the crescent moon
while the sky bled on the treetops
and the gunmen waited
with sunset staining their rifle-barrels
like the blood of a hunter's kill.

In that great stillness I came to you,

my lover, my sister, my wife.
In the stillness of a night that lasted a thousand years
I came down your path through the pale bushes,
past the willows that drank from the waterside.
In the stillness I followed your heartbeat
into the land of long reeds and the scented fern,
into a coolness green as the mist.

And when the blood had left the sky
and only the moon and stars were there to shed their old light,
we lay together on the earth that smelled of apples,
feeling its moistness, breathing its darkness,
secure in its heaviness,
the earth that had endured for aeons
in the silence before time.

One day I will go back.
One day when peace has come again
I will return to that village by the Drina,
and there I will walk down the moon-way
through the bushes by the riverside,
enter the invisible door,
and the trees will not be shredded with shells,
and no sudden stutter of gunshots
will come from across the water.

And there will be no screaming,
neither of slaughtered cattle nor raped women,
and no stamping of running feet,
no cursing, no smashing of glass,
no stink of war.

And I shall not find you in the meadow
beside Ludmilla, who had no head,
and Ahmad, beaten to death with rifle-butts.
I shall not find you on your back in a cloud of flies,
your legs spread-eagled,
and the earth still moist with your blood.

There will be so many things
I shall not find that day, Svetlana,
the tears will run back into my eyes
and the only sounds shall be
the running of the river over its white pebbles
and the turning of the earth
in silence
in a silence sharp as knives.

Granton Shore

It is hard to think that the sun
setting over Bosnia tonight
has set on you for ever,
and you will not be there
to greet its rising on the Drina,
nor Ahmad, nor little Ludmilla,
nor any of your people.

And though tonight I walk along the Granton shore
and see the glow of distant Mossmoran
and the coastal lights of Fife
pricking the darkness like gunfire,
there is no satisfaction in my heart
when I think of the aid we brought,
the food, the medicine, the absence of guns.

I wish I had been your soldier.
I wish I had been there to meet
those killers with a gun in my hand.
I wish I had killed for you,
I wish I had died for you
Svetlana, that you might have lived
with Ahmad and young Ludmilla
and all your people
to see the sun rise again and again
because it is oh, so good!

And though the last vile belch of communism
be no more than a bad memory,
and though the butcher of Belgrade
is being driven from his lair,
I cannot rejoice tonight
because my heart is with a massacred village,
and I see again the four-and-forty people
we found in that red field,
the four-and-forty we shovelled under the weeping earth.
And I cannot be reconciled
to the fact that the men who did it
are home tonight watching television,
and making love to their wives,
the men who raped you so brutally,
so many times,
then cut your fair throat.

Fat Dutch Woman

Today it's on file,
it's documented.
Today I can finally say it happened
{it did! I saw it!}
and no one will call me a liar,
and I will not call myself a liar, I will
not doubt what I saw, not
get tied up in endless hairsplitting about
appearance and reality, not think it
was all a nightmare or that I was
hallucinating hysterical feverish going ga-ga,
because today the War Crimes Commission
has it on record. Period.
They listened carefully, politely,
the tape-recorder whispered, they said
they'd heard worse
(!)
I kept my voice flat and tried
hard
not to weep buckets
as I transfigured back into sanity
letting all the pus ooze out of my brain
after three years festering there
surrounded by indifference
to nationalist/communist massacres,
deafened by the yawns of people who
don't know don't care and
worst of all
can't imagine what hell is like.
And I – haunted by hell for three years,
jumping whenever a door went slam bang,
viewing the antics of rock bands strutting
around in orgies of pseudo-evil – I who
had seen the real thing, knew
what it did, knew how unsexy death is
and how the dead stink like blocked toilets
they stink so, oh God! they stink,
and on a diet of righteous anger
I survived,

on guilt and anger
and a desire to see those criminals not just –
not just punished but wiped off the face of the earth
for ever and for ever –
I went out into the sunshine
of a strange spring afternoon
in a strange foreign city where I had never been before
and sat down at a round table under
an umbrella outside a small cafe,
and the world went about its business
just as though it didn't matter.
Cars sped by and tourist buses,
the pretty waitress brought my order,
and couples argued, and lovers held hands, and
a fat Dutch woman Rubens could have painted ate
ice-cream in a long glass with a cherry on top of it,
and tame sparrows picked around my feet
for crumbs from the table
and I couldn't hold back any more, no
I wept
wept
wept
and was politely ignored,
feeling neither anger nor guilt now,
just a sadness fading
into delicate blue ether,
bitter as cordite fumes,
endless as tears.

Glory

Wolfe at Quebec and Robert Clive
were the heroes I believed in
when I was a little boy hungry
for ice-cream cones and adventure.

They were the brave wild brothers
who had made our Empire,
the one on the Heights of Abraham
surrounded by vast forests,
the other at Plassey
in the midst of the elephants.

How I wanted our Empire back again
just so I could serve it, red-coated,
like Wolfe at Quebec and Robert Clive!
But courage when it came
wore a very different face.

I saw a little German guy in Bosnia
who was short, plump and mild,
with spectacles, not much hair,
and an office job somewhere safe.
But when the mortars opened up on us
he took his lorry down a road so hacked with fire
it looked like the very door of hell.
He went there, alone,
with splinters flying about his head
and the courage of many heroes in his heart.

I never knew his name.
He was no Wolfe, nor Robert Clive,
but because of that one man
a village of doomed people survived,
and I think that has more true glory
than many battles the redcoats won,
or the riches of the Indian Raj.

Remembering that Night

In this fifth winter of Bosnia's crucifixion the wind rose
and shook down the old hawthorn tree that stood
at the bottom of my garden. A cold wind,
a bitter wind it would be for the people
we had seen in shell-wracked Sarajevo
living without gas or electricity,
and with bits of cardboard tacked over the holes
where windows once were.

That same night
a man died in the Grassmarket, huddled
with his newspapers in the doorway of a boutique,
and is now either nothing or with the Lord in paradise
just as surely as if a bullet had drilled his brains out
in a famous fight on television.
He too is part of that night when the wind blew
and the tree fell.

Do you remember, said Joe,
the night we got lost in those damn mountains –
what were they called again? Yes, and we
hid the van in the trees and waited for the Chetniks
to come and kill us. Christ, the things you do for fun!

So we stretched our toes out to the fire
and reminisced about our mission, and the worst
things we had seen seemed gentle somehow
in the firelight and the warm room.

And only I know that Joe can't sleep
without the pills he takes, and he knows too
how I weep sometimes, even on bright sunny days,
weep until my whole body shakes.

Barley

We left men able to smile again
and women with tears of joy in their eyes.
We left children happy
and well-fed at last.
And bumping over the farm track
in our empty battered van,
we saw barley in the field
ripening over the graves
of last year's battles,
and stray stems already spouting
from the turned earth of yesterday's,
even those so fresh and shallow
that men's feet were sticking out –
even there the green was growing.

And,
despite everything,
despite it all,
the land purred with green joy
as we passed through,
and life flowed on and on.